This book is dedicated to
Ravioli Ross,
the worlds best dog.

Table of Contents

Introduction

I always knew Ravioli would write a book like this. I mean, the boy is always stopping to smell the flowers and wandering off on our hikes up into the mountains around Telluride to check out new plants. You can't keep him focussed on sticks or chasing squirrels like the rest of us dogs. And let's be honest, he's pretty well set up for just such a task with such small legs! So it makes perfect scents (yeah, I know, pretty "punny" for a dog but, I'm pretty darn sophisticated) that he'd write this guide to wildflowers and plants. He's definitely the expert dog around here when it comes to those kinds of things. So, read the book and get your inner Ravioli on when you head up into the mountains. Hopefully me and Ravs see you rooting around on all fours. Maybe we'll even play with a stick together too...or go for a swim...oooh yeah, and maybe a chase or two!? But if you want to stick with Ravioli and smell some flowers, I wouldn't blame you either.

Much Love,
Sedona Wise

Folklore and Medicinal Uses

Since the beginning of time, humankind has cultivated wildflowers and documented their medicinal benefits. The magic of the mountains can be told through wildflowers, many wildflowers behold their own folklore and legends. Wildflowers carry fascinating histories, some amazing, some amusing, and some very important. Even today many wildflowers behold a rich history of folklore and legend.

From strange and often dangerous herbal remedies to black magic and whimsical legends of love, wildflower folklore will not disappoint the curious mind. In this field guide, medicinal and poisonous properties of wildflowers meet untamed legends, histories and superstitions twist into the wild world of adventure; all included with the adorable adventure dog, Ravioli as a fearless leader on the quest to wildflower identification.

*We will not take any responsibility for any adverse effects from the use of plants. Always seek advice from a professional before using a plant medicinally. The * indicates that the plant may have toxic properties, until you are a confident botanist, it is best to assume that wildflowers contain levels of toxicity. The medicinal usage in this book is merely an opportunity to open your mind to the wondrous and fascinating usages that the natural world offers us.*

Ecology of The Colorado Rocky Mountains

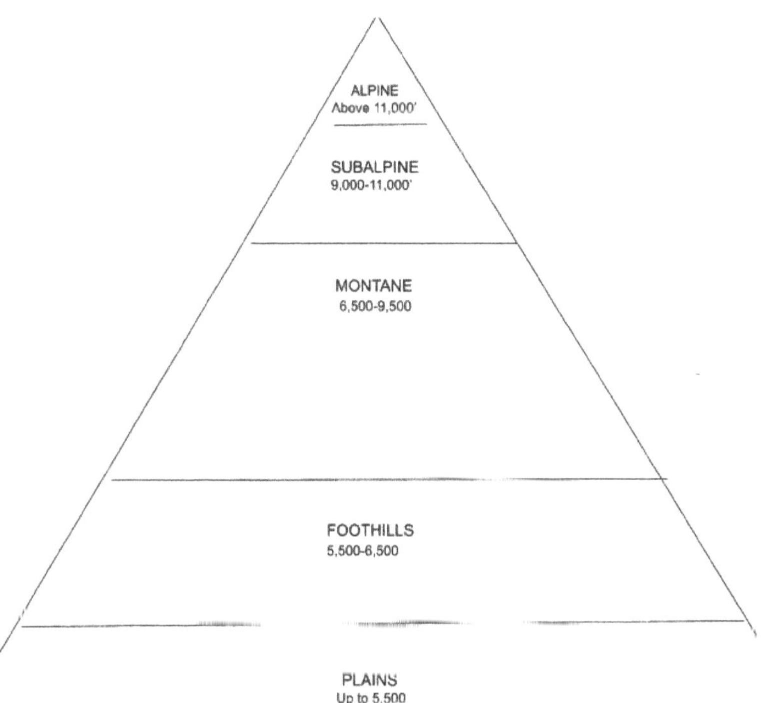

Anatomy of a Wildflower

The four major parts of a flower's reproductive system are the pistil, stamen, sepal, and petal. By observing the number, color, and arrangement of these parts you will be on your way identifying various wildflowers just like Ravioli.

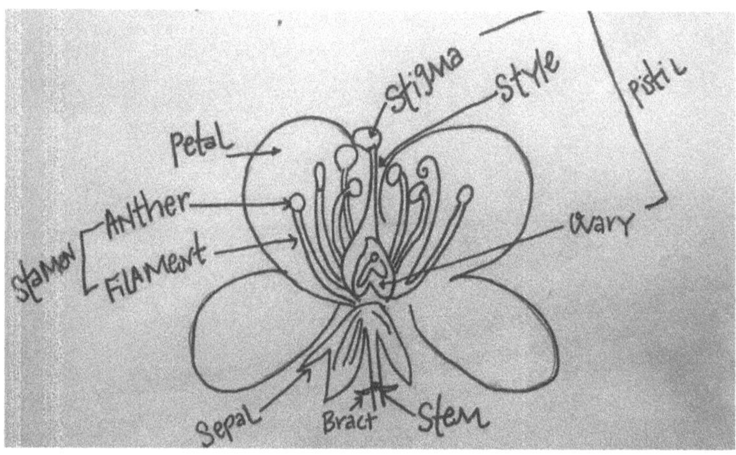

Inflorescence is the complete flower head of a plant and how it is arranged. In other words, it is the flower structure. This includes the stem, stalk, bracts and flowers. Raceme, panicle and umbel are common types of inflorescence.

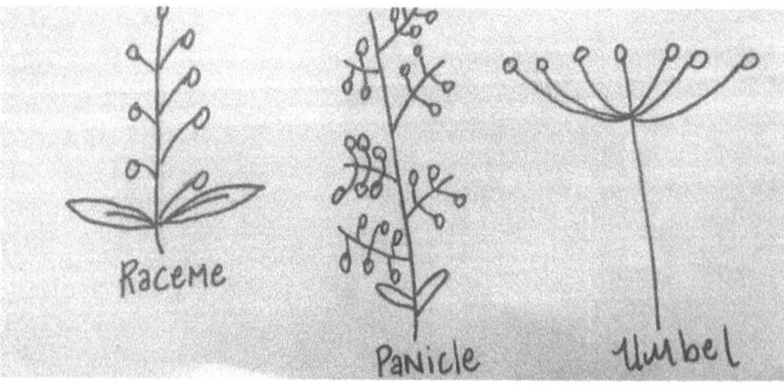

The leaves of a wildflower also help identify the flower. Common leaf shapes are: lance shaped, narrow, oval, palmately lobed, and toothed.

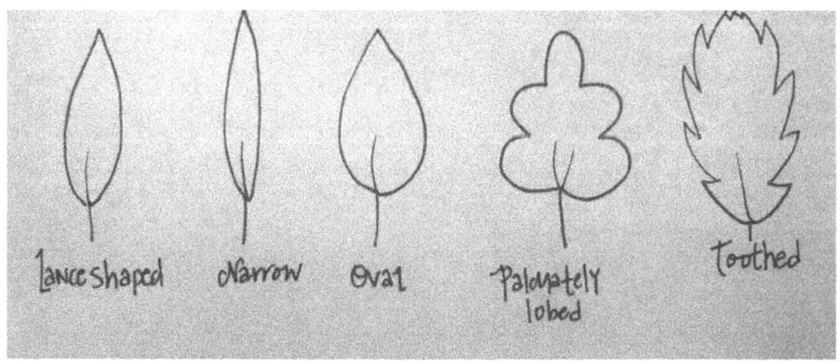

The arrangement of the leaves can also help identify wildflowers. Common arrangements are: alternate, basal, opposite, palmately compound, pinnately compound, and whorled.

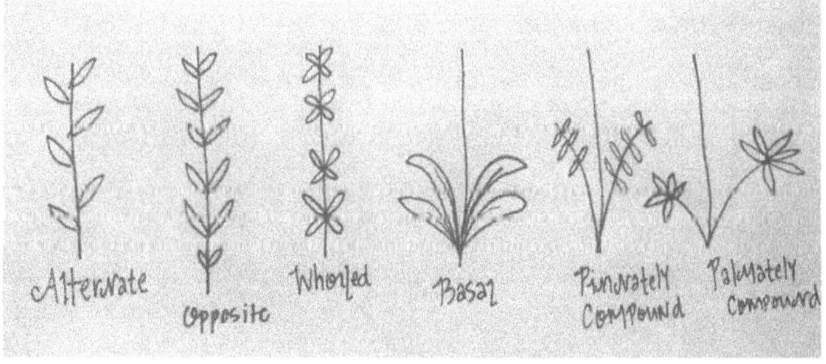

Aspen Daisy/Fleabane/Aster

Erigeron speciosus

Aster Family

Notes

Daisies are found on every continent except Antarctica. If you were a pocket gopher this may just be your favorite food!

Medicinal

This flower aids with digestive issues as it is a diuretic.

Scout it Out

This is an abundant flower found in open fields and meadows, on the edge of aspen clusters and in aspen groves, in both wet and dry habitats.

Season: June-September

Elevation: 2,000-12,000 ft

Description: Up to two inch wide Lavender flowers sit atop a stem made up of 1-5 inch basal leaves.

Blue Flax

Linum lewisii

Flax family

Season: May-September

Elevation: 3,500-11,000 ft

Description: Pale blue flowers bloom from the bottom upward. The 5 petals are about an inch to an inch and a half across and streaked with dark blue veins. Each stem produces several flowers.

Notes

History shows that flax has been used to make linen. Linen is the fabric that pharaohs were wrapped with in their tomb.

Medicinal

Decorate your next salad with this beauty; not only will it add color but it is packed with fiber and protein.

Scout it Out

This flower loves the sun! Find it in dry climates on disturbed hillsides.

Chiming Bells/Streamside Bluebells

Mertensia ciliata

Borage family

Notes

There are two common types of bell flowers, both symbolize everlasting love; gratitude and humility. The Bluebell's bulbs are extremely toxic, there is a belief that anyone who wanders into a ring of bluebells will fall under fairy enchantment and eventually die from.

Medicinal

*Toxic when consumed yet ingesting in moderation may balance PH levels.

Scout it Out

Find clusters of bells along stream sides or in open dry rocky regions where their clusters will be smaller and much shorter.

Season: Late May-July

Elevation: 6,000-12,500 ft

Description: The leaves of the bells are lance shaped while the nodding blue tubular flowers fade to pink.

Rocky Mountain Columbine

Aquilegia coerulea

Buttercup family

Season: Late June-September

Elevation: 5,000-13,700 ft

Description: This beaut can be observed in a variety of petal colors from deep purple to blue, pink yellow, and even white. It has five white sepals, and five petals with spurs extending behind the front petals.

Notes

In 1899 the stunning Rocky Mountain Columbine became Colorado's state flower. It is illegal to pick ANY part of the plant. In Colorado, picking a columbine is a punishable misdemeanor.

Medicinal

Do not harvest, but stop and smell it's delightful aroma.

Scout it Out

Find the columbine flower in both moist and rocky soils. From aspen groves to open meadows and up far above tree line the columbine is sure to put on a show.

Jacob's Ladder

Polemonium pulcherrimum

Phlox family

Notes

This adorable flower is named after the biblical story of a dream Jacob, son of Isaac had of a ladder ascending to heaven.

Medicinal

Harvest this flower in the summer and dry it to use for headache and fever relief.

Scout it Out

Find clusters of this flower in partly shaded regions and among a densely wooded floor.

Season: Late May-August

Elevation: 8,000-13,500 ft

Description: Leaves are long and fern like while the bell like flowers are small and blue-lavender.

Lupine

Lupinus argenteus

Pea family

Notes

This hybridizing species can be found in dry areas where it will be scattered and of a shorter variety. In more moist and wooded regions these beauties will grow tall to be a magnificent display of flora.

Medicinal

The plant can be made into herbal tea for diuretic, laxative and anti-inflammatory properties.

Scout it Out

Lupine grows in abundance. Find it in moist meadows, open fields, the forest's edge, and dry and rocky hillsides.

Season: May-September

Elevation: 4,600-10,600 ft

Description: Light blue pea-type flowers are ar ranged along a lanky stem. Narrow leaves radiate from a single point of attachment, they are palmately compound.

Monkshood

Aconitum Columbianum

Buttercup family

Season: July-August

Elevation: 1,000-12,500 ft

Description: Green stamens are surrounded by five inner petals that are smaller than the hood of the flower. There are small leaves along the stalk and larger multi lobed leaves near the bottom.

Notes

Monkshood gets its name from the shape of the back sepal of the flower which resembles the cowl (hood) of a monk's robe.

Medicinal

****Poisonous to both people and animals. Do not touch any part of the plant because it's toxins can be absorbed through the skin.

Scout it Out

You can find Monkshood in many moist regions of the rocky mountains.

Mountain Harebell

Campanula rotundifolia

Bellflower family

Season: June-September

Elevation: 5,000-13,500 ft

Description: The five flowers of the harebell are often nodding, but can be erect. They are around 4-15mm in length.

Notes

Scottish folklore says that fairies hide and cast spells among the bells to transform themselves into hares.

Medicinal

The leaves of the harebell are rich in Vitamin C. Or make a tonic for ear pain.

Scout it Out

From dry southwest facing slopes to moist northeast facing slopes you may catch a glimpse of the Mountain Harebell.

Parry's Gentian

Gentiana parryi

Gentianaceae Gnetian

Season: July-September

Elevation: 7,500-13,000 ft

Description: Before the flower unfolds, its petals swirl around each other. The sun opens it up to five rounded-or pointed petals.

Notes

This flower, along with many other nouns in nature are named after Charles Parry. He is one of the most known botanists of the 19th century. Parry was a highly respected and loved doctor, explorer, and naturalist.

Medicinal

*Make a tonic to relieve stomach aches and headaches.

Scout it Out

Along forest edges and into open meadows.

Silky Phacelia/Purple Fringe

Phacelia sericea

Waterleaf Family

Notes

Some plants have the ability to absorb the minerals around it. Silky Phacelia accumulates more gold deposits within its tissue than any other plant.

Medicinal

***Because Silky Phacelia has the power to accumulate minerals it can also take in the heavy metals around it. Best not to eat any part of the plant.

Scout it Out

Find this plant in forest clearings and high alpine tundra areas.

Season: June-August

Elevation: 8,500-13,500 ft

Description: There are many tiny purple flowers that are tightly packed along the stalk of this plant. Yellow stamens protrude out along the flowers. The leaves are finely divided and hairy.

Rocky Mountain Penstemon

Scrophulariaceae

Plantain family

Season: June-August

Elevation: 5,000-11,000 ft

Description: Look into the mouth of the two lobed upper and three lobed lower lips and you will notice fuzz protruding from its mouth. Its smooth leaves are narrow and alternate.

Notes

There are over sixty varieties of penstemon's native to Colorado and two hundred and fifty world-wide. It was once believed that Bearded Penstemon belonged to the Figwort family, taxonomy has proved otherwise.

Medicinal

Crush the flower to make a poultice to help heal bruising.

Scout it Out

In dry rocky regions you will be able to spot this brilliant blue/violet flower.

Sky Pilot

Polemonium Eximium

Phlox family

Season: Late June-August

Elevation: 11,000-13,700 ft

Description: Blue purple flowers with bright orange yellow stamens tightly clustered on the top of a tall stem. The fern-like leaves are divided into thick segments with whorls of small leaflets.

Notes

Sky Pilot is very similar to Jacob's Ladder. The big difference is the elevation in which it grows. This is a hearty high elevation plant found in high alpine rocky regions.

Medicinal

Unknown.

Scout it Out

Although a common plant, it is a special find as it takes work to find this flower. It grows only in high alpine regions. Look in rocky crevices for it's lavender to dark purple color.

Subalpine Larkspur

Delphinium barbeyi

Hellebore Family

Notes

Larkspur is very poisonous to dogs. It can cause muscle weakness, tremors, possibly paralysis and even death.

Medicinal

NONE! All parts of the plant are toxic. Merely touching the plant could cause skin irritations.

Scout it Out

Find these lanky flowers in aspen woodlands and moist regions along water sources in open fields.

Season: July-August

Elevation: 8,000-13,000 ft

Description: The flowers are made up of five distinct sepals and even one in the back of the flower making a spur. The leaves are toothed, large and divided.

Sugar Bowl/Vase Flower

Clematis hirsutissima

Buttercup family

Season: May-June

Elevation: 4,000-10,000 ft

Description: The leaves of this flower are long and narrow. They are divided several times and covered with fine hairs. The nodding bell shaped flower is dark purple It is covered in tiny silver hairs and has four leather like sepals and yellow stamens.

Notes

When hiking in spring, keep your eyes open for this beauty as it is one of the first blooms of the year-A sure sign that summer is coming and many more wildflowers are on the way.

Medicinal

Use the leaves to make a tea to relieve headaches and the root to alleviate nasal congestion.

Scout it Out

Among dry, disturbed soil in open hillsides and fields.

Towering Jacob's Ladder

Polemonium foliosissimum

Phlox Family

Season: June-August

Elevation: 6,000-13,000 ft

Description: Towering Jacob's Ladder grows up to three feet. The flower has five petals and five yellow stamens. The narrow leaves climb the stem creating a ladder.

Notes

The name of this flower comes from the biblical story where Jacob climbed a ladder to heaven. The leaves of this flower are symbolic of the ladder.

Medicinal

The root of this flower may be used to treat lung and breathing complications such as coughing.

Scout it Out

Jacob's Ladder grows in moist shaded meadows, often at the edge of the forest.

Vetch/Common American Vetch

Vicia americana

Pea family

Season: May-September

Elevation: 7,500-13,000 ft

Description: Smooth, oblong leaflets are tipped to a small, sharp point. The flowers are very small, purplish to magenta and occur singly or as pairs.

Notes

American vetch is drought tolerant, it is great for the soil as it attracts and strengthens nitrogen.

Medicinal

Use for treating skin issues. Vetch has antiseptic properties when used externally it can help with many skin issues such as eczema.

Scout it Out

Vetch grows in a variety of locations ranging from swampy woodlands to dry arid meadows.

Western Blue Virginsbower

Clematis occidentalis

Buttercup family

Season: May-June

Elevation: 8,000-11,000 ft

Description: One pale purplish-pink maybe even blue-violet bell-shaped flower sits at the end of each vine. The leaves are divided into three thick leaflets.

Notes

The seed floss is very flammable, thus it makes excellent tinder for starting fires.

Medicinal

ALL PARTS ARE POISONOUS!

Scout it Out

Find it from foothills to montane zone in moist to dry soil in wooded to open areas.

Whipple's Penstemon

Penstemon Whippleanus

Figwort family

Season: June-August

Elevation: 8,000-13,000 ft

Description: Long, thick and leathery basal leaves lead up to a deep maroon penstemon that appears to have tiny silver hairs.

Notes

This flower was named in honor of topographical engineer and Civil War General, Amiel Weeks Whipple. He surveyed possible routes for the Transcontinental Railroad.

Medicinal

The root of the penstemon can be made into a tea to relieve toothaches.

Scout it Out

This species grows in montane, subalpine, and alpine forests.

Arrowleaf Senecio/Ragwort

Senecio triangularis

Aster family

Season: June-September

Elevation: 6,000-12,500 ft

Description: The leaves are triangular. They look like an arrow head and have sharp teeth and have branched yellow flower heads.

Notes

Elk and deer find this flower to be a tasty treat. However, there is a cost to eating too much of it. This plant contains naturally occurring toxins which may cause vomiting and liver damage.

Medicinal

***It is reported that the Cheyenne Tribe cultivated this plant's roots to make tea with the hopes of alleviating chest pain. However, note that there is a toxic limit.

Scout it Out

Look for this yellow flower in moist areas such as the banks of streams.

Butter and Eggs Toadflax

Linaria vulgaris

Figwort family

Season: June-September

Elevation: 4,600-10,600 ft

Description: Two tone yellow flowers with an upper and lower lip. The upper lip has two lobes while the lower lip has three lobes with an orange patch on it, it has numerous gray green narrow leaves.

Notes

Folklore states that if you walk around this beauty three times it will rid any spell cast on you.

Medicinal

Can be made into a tea to be used as a diuretic or laxative.

Scout it Out

This happy flower thrives in disturbed dirt especially on dry hillsides.

Dalmatian Toadflax

Linaria dalmatica

Figwort family

Notes

This flower is a favorite of Ravioli's, yet it is considered an invasive weed. A single plant can produce a half million seeds for a solid five years.

Medicinal

None to note.

Scout it Out

This tall and cheery plant thrives in disturbed dirt among dry hillsides.

Season: June-September

Elevation: 4,600-10,600 ft

Description: This plant has fern-like leaves and a yellow flower, a penstemon-like mouth and pinkish cheeks.

Dwarf Sunflower

Helianthus pumilus

Aster Family

Season: July-September

Elevation: 6,000-9,000 ft

Description: Showy yellow 1-3 inch flowers sit atop a branched stem. The leaves of this sunflower are lance shaped, thick and rough.

Notes

Sunflower buds face east in morning as the sun rises and continues to face the sun as it travels throughout the sky.

Medicinal

Sunflower oil is a great source of Vitamin D.

Scout it Out

Find the Dwarf Sunflower on hillsides and roadsides, from the foothills to mid montane forest.

Fernleaf Lousewort

Pedicularis bracteosa

Broomrape family

Season: July and August

Elevation: 8,000-13,000 ft

Description: This plant has delicate, fern-like basal leaves that range from 12"-24". It's stem is topped by an arrangement of light yellow to red streaked, beaked flowers.

Notes

Folklore states that this plant has the ability to make people fall in love due to its seductive properties.

Medicinal

****Lousewort can absorb toxins from neighboring plants. It is best not to harvest this plant.

Scout it Out

This towering plant lives in shaded sub alpine woods.

Heartleaf Arnica

Arnica Cordifolia

Aster family

Season: June-August

Elevation: 4,600-10,600 ft

Description: The leaves are alternating and heart shaped, Its flower is made of relatively ten ray like petals, look closely they are notched at the tips.

Notes

With its large heart shaped leaves and roughly ten proud bright petals the Heartleaf Arnica is perhaps the easiest yellow aster to identify.

Medicinal

One can make an ointment from the flower (which contains arnicin) to help ease bruising. The roots may be made into a tea to help with inflammation.

Scout it Out

This flower is common in moist montane and subalpine forests. It is much taller in open areas while in shaded regions it is shorter and its leaves create more of a blanket covering the understory.

Many Flowered Puccoon/Stoneseed

Lithospermum multiflorum

Forget-Me-Not family

Notes

The Many Flowered Puccoon has both male and female parts, thus can self produce.

Medicinal

unknown

Scout it Out

This flower grows in dry wooded subalpine regions.

Season: June-September

Elevation: 6,000-9,500 ft

Description: This small yellow flower beholds five petals in the shape of a trumpet. The basal leaves alternate closely together at the stem.

Old Man on The Mountain

Hymenoxys grandiflora

Aster Family

Season: June-August

Elevation: 8,500-14,000 ft

Description: Thin linear leaves climb a thick stem. It is wooly where the stem meets the flower head. The inch to two inch petals are thin and sometimes droopy.

Notes

There are over 200 species of Sunflower and Old Man on The Mountain is one of them. However it is set apart because of its non-conformity wisdom. It is characteristic of sunflowers to turn toward the sun as it moves through the day. However, Old Man on The Mountain will nearly always continue to face East.

Medicinal

Prepare the root into a poultice to aid skin rashes and sores.

Scout it Out

Find this old man on many of your high alpine hikes. It is set apart by its hairy backside.

Orange Agoseris

Agoseris aurantiaca

Aster Family

Notes

There are few orange wildflowers, so when you see an orange agoseris relish in the rare color experience delight you are encountering.

Medicinal

**Enjoy the top of this flower on salads or make a tea to help with overall inflammation. The leaves contain a number of nutrients including iron, zinc, boron, calcium, silicon, and are especially high in potassium. It is also high in vitamins A, B complex, C, and D. Take caution as some reports claim levels of toxicity.

Scout it Out

Find this coppery orange flower in meadows and rocky fields.

Season: June-August

Elevation: 5,500-12,500 ft

Description: This aster has pointed tips at the end of it's flower petals. Also note the cluster of basal leaves.

Orange Sneezeweed/Owl's Claws

Hymenoxys hoopesii

Aster family

Notes

In Greek mythology, Helenium (sneezeweed) was thought to emerge from the tears of Helen of Troy.

Medicinal

A snuff made from the crushed blossoms and the leaves can be inhaled in the treatment of head-aches and hay fever.

Scout it Out

In moist open meadows and along the side of moist trails.

Season: June-August

Elevation: 6,500-11,500 ft

Description: Oblong leaves sit atop a stout stem. The leaves are lanceolate or narrow and alternate along the stem.

Shrubby Cinquefoil

Pentaphylloides floribunda

Rose family

Notes

Medieval folklore believed cinquefoil to be a lucky plant. According to folklore cinquefoil can bring luck in one of these five realms: love, wisdom, health, wealth, and/or power. In medieval times dried cinquefoil was hung above doors or put into empty egg shells to protect the home from negativity and bring good luck.

Medicinal

Create a tea or tincture from the leaves of this flower to remedy several ailments such as stomach cramps, uncomfortable skin conditions, tooth aches, and gout.

Scout it Out

Find this yellow flower in high alpine meadows and moist areas. It is also found in the foothills and subalpine meadows.

Season: June-September

Elevation: 4,600-10,600 ft

Description: Copy This shrub is composed of narrow leaflets that are pinnately compound. The flower has five round petals.

Western Wallflower

Erysimum Capitatum

Mustard family

Notes

This flower is an excellent pollinator. It has been observed that it's anthers will curl backward after pollen has been released.

Medicinal

Create a poultice from the flower to alleviate bronchial congestion.

Scout it Out

Find this flower anywhere from the plains to high alpine meadows, it will even grow in rocky regions.

Season: May-August

Elevation: 3,500-13,500 ft

Description: Four, four inch petals are arranged on a stem with long narrow leaves.

Yellow Monkey Flower

Mimulus guttatus

Figwort family

Notes

The shape of the Monkey Flower is supposed to resemble a monkey's face.

Medicinal

Boil the plant to make an infusion for your bath, it will help alleviate soreness and bruising.

Scout it Out

This flower grows on rocky slopes where moisture is abundant.

Season: May-September

Elevation: 5,500-9,500 ft

Description: The flowers are yellow with red spots in the throat. It's leaves are oval-shaped, the upper leaves lack stems while lower leaves have long, tube stems.

Yellow Salsify/Shepherd's Clock

Tragopogon dubius major

Aster family

Notes

The Yellow Salsify has numerous aliases such as: Goatsbeard, Oysterplant, Shepherd's Clock, Noon Flower, and Jack-go-to-bed-at-noon.

Medicinal

Ingest this flower to be used as a diuretic, it may aid digestion and an upset stomach.

Scout it Out

Find this happy flower among ditches and roadsides. Or venture into the woods and it can be found in open fields.

Season: May-July

Elevation: 3,000-10,500 ft

Description: From the stem, this aster's leaves are long and narrow while the flower is composed of a variety of rays. The outer rays are long while the inner rays are short.

Yellow Stonecrop

Amerosedum lanceolatum

Stonecrop family

Notes

Because the leaves are succulent and the roots spread this flower, one can be creative and use it for a variety of green landscaping and gardening projects.

Medicinal

Use topically to treat skin ailments such as rashes, warts and other dermatitis conditions.

Scout it Out

Find stonecrop in dry open rocky locations. Look for it on your higher elevation hikes sprouting from rocky soil.

Season: May-August

Elevation: 3,500-13,000 ft

Description: Five pointed petals make up the small flower as does ten stamens. The succulent leaves are narrow and alternate.

Alpine Clover

Trifolium dasyphyllum

Pea family

Season: June-August

Elevation: 7,500-13,000 ft

Description: The petals of this flower extend into long and narrow pointed lobes with a leafless hairy stem and three lancelot leaves.

Notes

There are 95 species of clover in the United States. Clovers are considered good luck. It was common for medieval Christians to wear a locket of dried clover around their necks to protect them from evil spirits and ward off the charms cast by witches.

Medicinal

Create a tea of dried clover to help detox your blood and support kidney function.

Scout it Out

You can find this flower growing in high alpine exposed, rocky areas.

Elephant's Head

Pedicularis groenlandica

Broomrape family

Season: June-August

Elevation: 7,500-13,500 ft

Description: The leaves are sharp and fernlike. The top half of the stalk will flower with many small flowers that resemble the trunk and ears of an elephant's head.

Notes

There is no other flower in the Rockies shaped like this beauty. Look closely, the stalk really does look like it is covered with tiny elephant heads!

Medicinal

Make a tincture to aid muscle cramps and muscle pains.

Scout it Out

Find this whimsical flower in subalpine wet woodlands and meadows.

Fireweed

Chamerion angustifolium

Evening Primrose family

Season: July-September

Elevation: 5,000-12,000 ft

Description: Four flow-ered magenta petals climb a tall stem. The lance shaped leaves alternate, along the stem.

Notes

Fireweed earned its name from being a byproduct of wildfires. This wildflower colonizes after a wildfire takes on the land. Folklore states that when the top flowers bloom, the first snow is a mere 6 weeks away.

Medicinal

*Cautiously use fireweed as a tonic for pain and swelling. Fireweed is high in manganese which helps balance hormones.

Scout it Out

You can find fireweed among dis-turbed soil, near streams, in forests and meadows.

Fairy Trumpet/Scarlet Gilia

Ipomopsis Aggregata

Phlox family

Notes

Use your imagination to create a scenario where you can hear the fairies blowing their trumpets for you as you saunter through the glorious mountainside.

Medicinal

Make a poultice with the whole plant and apply to rheumatic joints to ease inflammation or create an infusion from its roots and use as a laxative.

Scout it Out

Find this trumpet along roadsides and hillsides in dry disturbed soil.

Season: June-September

Elevation: 6,500-10,500 ft

Description: A bright red trumpet shaped flower with 5 pointed lobes are arranged along the top of a long stem, it's pinnately divided leaves alternate at it's base.

King's Crown

Rhodiola integrifolia

Stonecrop family

Season: July-September

Elevation: 5,000-12,000 ft

Description: One inch long leaves alternatively climb the stem to the bright red flowering crown of this plant.

Notes

King's Crown is a succulent-it has water storing leaves therefore it can survive with minimal water.

Medicinal

Do not consume in large quantities. In smaller doses King's Crown is an anti-inflammatory that can help alleviate toothache and ear pain.

Scout it Out

Find King's Crown on your high alpine hikes in both moist and dry rocky areas.

Narrowleaf/Wyoming Paintbrush

Chamerion angustifolium

Figwort family

Season: June-September

Elevation: 5,000-11,000 ft

Description: Relative to this paintbrushes counterparts, the narrowleaf can be distinguished by its narrow bracts.

Notes

This fauna hybridizes, thus there are nearly 200 species of various colored paintbrush flora worldwide. The Wyoming Paintbrush can grow up to three feet tall.

Medicinal

May use in small doses for rheumatism due to it's selenium content.

Scout it Out

Paintbrush species are found in abundance in most mountain regions. The narrow leaf is commonly found in elevations up to 11,000ft.

Parry's Primrose

Primula parryi

Primrose Family

Notes

Primrose is the symbol of safety and protection. Once upon a time it was placed on the doorstep to encourage fairies to bless the house and anyone living in it. Create a string of primrose on the first of May-or when spring first comes to your town to offer protection from evil fairies.

Medicinal

Dry the leaves and make an astringent to ease inflammation.

Scout it Out

Keep an eye out in boggy marshes on your high alpine hikes for this primrose.

Season: June-August

Elevation: 9,000-14,000 ft

Description: This Primrose has large upward lance shaped leaves at the base of its stem. There are no leaves along the stem which nods and beholds 3-10 five petal flowers.

Red Clover

Trifolium Pratense

Pea Family

Season: May-October

Elevation: 4,000-10,000 ft

Description: The red clover is generally low to the ground with three leafed clovers.

Notes

Fairies help guide bees to the rich pollen of the red clover.

Medicinal

The flowering tops are used for a variety of medicinal purposes. Make a tea to combat respiratory problems, detoxify blood, and help with menopausal side effects.

Scout it Out

This clover can be found in disturbed or undisturbed soils and throughout open areas of the Rocky Mountains.

Rosy Paintbrush

Castilleja rhexifolia

Broomrape Family

Season: June-September

Elevation: 8,500-13,500 ft

Description: Paintbrush leaves are lanceolate and up to 6 inches long. The cluster of colorful bracts have 3 long veins.

Notes

There are more than two hundred species of paintbrush in the Rocky Mountains.

Medicinal

Create a tea from the flower to help ease rheumatism.

Scout it Out

Most paintbrush varieties grow all over the western United states, the rosy variety is found in higher elevations in alpine meadow and on alpine slopes.

Shooting Star Columbine

Aquilegia elegantula

Buttercup family

Notes

The shooting Star Columbine is a relative to Colorado's majestic state flower, the Columbine. This Columbine species is hermaphrodite meaning it has both male and female organs and is self-fertile.

Medicinal

When chewed it may relieve ailments such as involuntary muscle spasms as well as overactive glands.

Scout it Out

You may find this Columbine species in moist shaded montane and subalpine forests.

Season: May-August

Elevation: 6,000-12,000 ft

Description: Five red petals appear to spire off the yellow stamen, giving It the appearance of a shooting star. In addition there are also five red and yellow sepals.

Twinberry Honeysuckle

Lonicera involucrata

Honeysuckle family

Notes

The Twinberry Honeysuckle is a conservationist! It is important for erosion control and restoration of riparian ecosystems from coastline to mountains. Legend has it that Honeysuckle is a symbol of fidelity and affection. Those who wear honeysuckle flowers are said to be able to dream of their true love.

Medicinal

**** Do not consume, the berries range from mildly toxic to poison-ous when ingested by humans.

Scout it Out

Finding this shrub should be sim-ple. Take a stroll along a river or up to a lake and you should find this honeysuckle plant.

Season: July-August

Elevation: 6,000-12,000 ft

Description: Small, tubular yellow flowers grow in pairs surrounded by two leafy bracts. It's bracts turn from green to dark red in late summer as its fruit ripens. This is a shrub that can grow up to twelve feet.

Wild Rose

Rosa woodsii

Rose family

Notes

The Wild Rose is related to apples, pears, apricots and other orchard fruits.

Medicinal

Wild roses aid inflammation. They also have around 40x the concentration of Vitamin C than oranges.

Scout it Out

Find this rose in dry open forests among disturbed soil.

Season: May- September

Elevation: 3,000-12,000 ft

Description: Five round pedals with the middle made up of yellow stamens and pistils. It has compound leaves that have toothed edges.

Bistort and Alpine Bistort

Bistorta vivipara

Buckwheat family

Google "Bistort health benefits" and you will find over two dozen different bistort remedies!

Alpine bistort varies from bistort in that it has a red detail off the base of the white sepals.

Bistort contains tannins, the entire plant may be used for a variety of ailments.

Find Bistort in moist subalpine and alpine meadows. It will most likely grow taller than the vegetation around it.

Season: June-August

Elevation: 8,500-14,000 ft

Description: The flower is very dense, it has tiny cylindrical flowers with five white sepals.

Alpine Spring Beauty

Claytonia megarhiza

Purslane family

Notes

"The Spring Beauty" is a Native American story about children seeing the Alpine Spring Beauty and joyfully welcoming this plant as the first blossoms of spring.

Medicinal

The roots of this flower can be dried and made into a tea to help with the common cold.

Scout it Out

Find this plant in high alpine rocky regions. It likes shelter, so look out for it in rocky crevices.

Season: July-August

Elevation: 9,500-13,500 ft

Description: Low to the ground thick round leaves protect the five white petals of this flower. The Flower also has two green sepals and red veins.

Canada Violet

Viola scopulorum

Violet family

Notes

Roman Mythology states that violets are that of Io's tears. Tears from a broken heart because she could not be with the God she fell in love with; Zeus.

Medicinal

A tea made from the plant's roots may be made to treat stomach pain.

Scout it Out

In moist shady areas from the foothills to the montane forest you may be lucky enough to lay eyes on this delicate beauty.

Season: May-July

Elevation: 9,500-13,500 ft

Description: This flower has five white shaped petals, the bottom one is pointed. Look for it's yellow center and purple veins. It's leaves are heart shaped

Cow Parsnip/Mother Dies

Heracleum sphondylium montanum

Parsley family

Fairy colonies are said to gather under the giant umbels to wait out rainstorms. Take a look if you are caught in a rainstorm and see the tall flowering plant towering the forest foliage and you just may spot a fairy. The origin of the name Mothers Dies comes from folklore; children were told that if they picked cow parsley, their mother would die-a threat intended to deter children from accidentally picking the ever so poisonous hemlock which resembles Cow Parsnip.

Medicinal

With caution, when brewed it may ward off mosquitos.

Scout it Out

Spot this giant in moist wooded areas as well as moist open meadows.

Season: June-August

Elevation: 5,000-11,000 ft

Description: This flower can grow to a grand 8 feet tall and has a huge flat umbel (umbrella) top with tiny white flowers. Cow Parsnip has giant 3 toothed lobed leaves.

Death Camas

Anticlea elegans

False Hellebore family

Notes

This plant contains zygadenine, perhaps a property more poisonous than strychnine.

Medicinal

****DO NOT HARVEST! This plant is named a Death Cama for a specific reason, it is very poisonous

Scout it Out

This flower can be found from sub-alpine to alpine moist meadows and open wooded areas.

Season: June-August

Elevation: 7,000-13,000 ft

Description: White flowers are near the top of it's 8-18" stem. The flowers are made up of six pointed stars, each point with a green spot near the center. The leaves of Death Camas are long and linear basal leaves.

Cutleaf Evening Primrose

Oenothera coronopifolia

Evening Primrose family

Season: May-August

Elevation: 4,500-10,000 ft

Description: Four white heart shaped petals with yellow stamens sit atop a stem. The plant has basal leaves that taper to a point.

Notes

Evening Primrose will last only one day. It will bloom in the evening and by mid morning it will have turned pink and withered away. Folklore says that fairies collect dew from the evening primrose and use it for their magic potions.

Medicinal

Use evening primrose as an herbal remedy for unpleasant skin conditions such as eczema and acne.

Scout it Out

You can find evening primrose among dry disturbed soil.

Globeflower

Trollius albiflorus

Buttercup family

Notes

This flower is often confused for a Marsh Marigold, as it's habitats are the same and they look so similar. However, look closely at the globeflower and you will notice that it is taller than the Marsh Marigold and has a greater number of sepals.

Medicinal

This plant is high in Vitamin C. Add it to a salad for a vitamin C boost.

Scout It Out

Find this flower in wet subalpine meadows and wet marshy alpine areas.

Season: June-August

Elevation: 7,500-13,500 ft

Description: The leaves of this plant are palmate and cut deeply, the Globeflower has 5-9 white petal like sepals.

Mariposa Lily/Gunnison Mariposa Lily

Calochortus gunnisonii

Lily family

Notes

The Gunnison Mariposa Lily earned its name from being first recorded by a botanist on the fatal Gunnison Expedition- a 19th century railroad expedition.

Medicinal

The Mariposa Lily has a hearty edible bulb. When ingested internally it may treat rheumatic swellings.

Scout it Out

Look for this delicate charmer in dry, open meadows, especially after a winter of heavy snowfall.

Season: March-July

Elevation: 5,000-11,000 ft

Description: Three often white, but can be pink, or purple petals form to create this delicate beauty. It's oblong anthers are yellow or pink in color and it has narrow, linear, basal leaves.

Frasera speciosa

Gentian family

Season: June-September

Elevation: 6,000-12,500 ft

Description: The leaves of this plant are long and narrow. It will only flower once in its life but when it does there are an abundance of 4 greenish white spotted petals with four curved stamens along the stalk.

Notes

This plant is one of the tallest flowering plants in the Rocky Mountains, it can grow up to 8 feet. It takes several years to grow, up to eighty years! It will only flower once, then it dies forever.

Medicinal

**Make a tea from the roots to help ease the following ailments: asthma, the common cold, and even stomach aches. Do not over consume as large quantities are toxic.

Scout It Out

Find this colossal plant in open areas all the way up to the forest's edge.

Mountain Pea

Lathyrus lanszwertii

Pea family

Notes

There are two common varieties of Pea flowers in the Rocky Mountains.

Medicinal

****Poisonous! This plant can cause muscle spasms and a weak heart beat.

Scout it Out

Peavines sprawl across the forest floor in the montane forest. Look for it on your wooded adventures along the trails edge.

Season: May-August

Elevation: 7,000-10,000 ft

Description: The pea-like flowers are white to creamy pink in color. They have purple lines radiating from the center, they grow in groups of two to ten with compound leaves.

Richardson's Geranium

Achillea lanulosa

Geranium family

Description: This flower has five rounded petals with deep veins. It's leaves are divided, and grow around the base, then arc in spaced intervals up the stem.

Notes

This plant is an excellent insect repellent. If you find yourself in a mosquito infested area, crush the petals up to expel the oil.

Medicinal

Make a tea from dried geranium leaves to help heal bruises, cuts and scrapes, eczema.

Scout it Out

You can find this flower in abundance in moist woodland areas.

Marsh Marigold

Caltha leptosepala

Buttercup family

English folklore believes that this marigold protects against evil fairies.

**** Toxic!

Find this flower in wet subalpine meadows in early spring or later in the summer in alpine wet areas.

Season: June-August

Elevation: 9,000-12,500 ft

Description: On this plant, the flowers have no real petals, the 5-15 se-pals look like petals. Yellow stamens brighten it's center, it's leaves are broad heart shaped or oblong.

Yarrow

Achillea millefolium

Daisy family

Notes

Yarrow is found all over the northern hemispheres and can be used as an insecticide.

Medicinal

Chew on the leaves to reduce toothaches or make a tonic of it to reduce fevers and headaches. *Pregnant women shall not take Yarrow as it may relax the uterus.

Scout it Out

You can find this flower in abundance throughout the Rocky Mountains.

Season: June-September

Elevation: 5,000-11,000 ft

Description: Five white rays and a yellow disk make up part of the tiny white flowers of Yarrow which umbel on a thin stem. The leaves of Yarrow resemble feathers because of their long pinnately dissected thin leaflets.

Index

About the Author(s)

Ravioli lives in Telluride, Colorado with his owner
Lauren Ross. Lauren adopted Ravioli in September
2006 from Table Mesa Animal Shelter, a small shelter
at the base of the Rocky Mountains in Arvada,
Colorado which was absorbed by what is now,
Foothills Animal Shelter in Golden, Co. Ravioli spent
his first four years living in Breckenridge, Colorado
where he fell in love spending his days outdoors and
following his nose. The duo then moved to Denver,
Colorado where Ravioli enjoyed the perks of city
life such as becoming a couch potato. He puffed up
in Denver due to lack of adventuring but not lack of
kibble and treats. After living in the confines of the city,
the two moved to Telluride in 2016 where they now call
home. In 2019 when Ravioli was 13 he was diagnosed
with cancer. Upon his recovery, he realized life is too
short and wanted to live his best life. This wildflower
guide blossomed out of his desire to be with nature
and his refusal to grow old and crotchety...he is now
15 years old and still enjoying his field work.

A Special thanks to all of Ravioli's hiking friends, especially those of you who have stayed out far longer than anticipated on our adventure to help find Ravioli when his nose gets the best of him. To Olivia Pedersen for all of your technical support. To Dan Noel for writing the witty intro for this book.